T0193270

# Our Dear Little One

## A letter from Mommy and Daddy

### By Anna Nolan

Copyright © 2024 Anna Nolan.

All rights reserved. No part of this book may be used or reproduced by any means, graphic, electronic, or mechanical, including photocopying, recording, taping or by any information storage retrieval system without the written permission of the author except in the case of brief quotations embodied in critical articles and reviews.

WestBow Press books may be ordered through booksellers or by contacting:

WestBow Press
A Division of Thomas Nelson & Zondervan
1663 Liberty Drive
Bloomington, IN 47403
www.westbowpress.com
844-714-3454

Because of the dynamic nature of the Internet, any web addresses or links contained in this book may have changed since publication and may no longer be valid. The views expressed in this work are solely those of the author and do not necessarily reflect the views of the publisher, and the publisher hereby disclaims any responsibility for them.

Any people depicted in stock imagery provided by Getty Images are models, and such images are being used for illustrative purposes only.
Certain stock imagery © Getty Images.

ISBN: 979-8-3850-1467-5 (sc)
979-8-3850-1469-9 (hc)
979-8-3850-1468-2 (e)

Library of Congress Control Number: 2023923854

Print information available on the last page.

WestBow Press rev. date: 01/15/2024

WESTBOW
PRESS®
A DIVISION OF THOMAS NELSON
& ZONDERVAN

# Our Dear Little One

## A letter from Mommy and Daddy

### By Anna Nolan

You are getting so big our dear little one!

You are strong, brave, smart, and a whole
lot of fun.

As you keep growing and learning each day,
Remember these three things that we have
to say.

Remember that Mommy and Daddy
love you,

8

No matter what you think, say, or do.

Remember Jesus loves you more than
we can.

He loves you so much there are scars on
his hands.

14

Remember that Jesus is the only way.
To be happy you must trust in Him and obey.

16

Things to remember One, Two and, Three.
We love you, God loves you, so live joyfully!

You are our dear one... you always will be!
We are so proud of you! Love, Mommy
and Daddy

Printed in the United States
by Baker & Taylor Publisher Services